I0176728

The Mindful Art of Verandaku

Micro Poems in a Macro World
Volume 1

Including an essay and how-to guide for your creative project

With selected images

縁側句

Jay Verney

ZEN KETTLE BOOKS | BRISBANE, QLD

Zen Kettle Books

Email: steaming@zenkettle.com
www.zenkettle.com

Publisher's Note: This is a work of poetry and non-fiction. Names, characters, places, and incidents may be a product of the author's imagination. Locales and public names are sometimes used for atmospheric purposes. Any resemblance to actual people, living or dead, or to businesses, companies, events, institutions, or locales is completely coincidental.

Book Cover Design: © Zen Kettle Design at zenkettle.com
Cover Image: Shorncliffe Pier, Qld, 2006 by VernLaw Images.
Book Layout © 2015 BookDesignTemplates.com

National Library of Australia Cataloguing-in-Publication entry

Author: Verney, Jay.
Title: The mindful art of verandaku: micro poems in a macro
          world – volume 1.
Subjects:Poetry.
          Poetry, Modern—21st century.

Dewey No: A821.4

ISBN 978-0-9945470-0-2

TABLE OF CONTENTS

AUTHOR NOTE

This is Volume One of *The Mindful Art of Verandaku*, a collection of poems which began life on the blog Veranda Life (www.verandalife.com) as the project *999 Verandakus*. The blog includes images for each of the poems, so if you'd like to see the full visual side of this project, you can check it out there. However, there are selected images included in this volume, too. The poems are based on traditional haiku, though with a broader range of subjects. I hope you'll enjoy them and, if you like, use them as mindful meditations when you need a little calm time. Volume 1 offers the first 333 of the 999 and, to begin, an essay, *The Verandaku Project*, which is about verandas, breathing, the power of now, and how to create your own poetic memoir with micro poems in a macro world.

Breathe ~ Relax ~ Drink Black Tea Often

For Lorrie

Life is a dessert
Ridiculous Colourful
Black tea tempers it

Verandaku: Haiku's daughter with a twist of minty fresh mango madness.

Prescription (mindful not medical): Contemplate 1 Verandaku 3 times daily with your beverage of choice and 10 minutes.

Prescription (creative not controlling): Capture a Verandaku daily (or at your leisure) on your walk, in the yard, the shower, the car, wherever you are in the moment.

The Verandaku Project

縁側句 事業

Saturday sunset
A dreamcalling veranda
Citronella melts

In the beginning ...

... was the breath. Of course, you say, of course.

And my breath was a little ragged, mostly from anxiety and stress and all those other words that mean anxiety and stress – they know who they are. I wasn't well, grasshopper. I was quite unwell, in fact, with a discombobulation and dysfunction of the balance – the mechanism that keeps you upright and travelling a straight line – that refused to heal itself except by barely noticeable tiny, teeny tiny degrees over a very long time. It was more than annoying.

I needed to take a breath and determine how I was to live my life without losing my mental balance as well. I did a few things, things that people prone to writing tend to do. I began a novel and eventually completed and published it (*Spawned Secrets*, another story for another day, of process, habit and breathing). I began a couple of blogs, as you do. One of them I called *Veranda Life*. At first, I wasn't sure what I would do there, but I knew it would aim to at least fulfill its motto or tagline, as they say in blogworld: *Breathe ~ Relax ~Drink Black Tea Often.*

These seemed like good things to do on the road to lessening anxiety and stress. I reminded myself, and any reader (or cat, for that matter) who happened by: *You breathe alone, and you breathe with every other living entity on and above the planet. Who is breathing in unison with you now? You can be certain that the pairs of lungs exactly synchronised with yours are in the millions, and more, and they're everywhere around the world, human and animal, fish and bird. Let's take a breath and think about that for an inhalation or two.*

We're breathing, we're alive, we could do worse, I thought, than take notice of Tennyson in his wonderful poem, *Ulysses,* in which the hero reminds us that we have to live our lives, regardless of obstacles:

> *I am a part of all that I have met;*
> *Yet all experience is an arch wherethro'*
> *Gleams that untravell'd world, whose margin fades*
> *For ever and for ever when I move*
> *How dull it is to pause, to make an end,*
> *To rust unburnish'd, not to shine in use!*
> *As tho' to breathe were life.*

I couldn't see myself sitting in a corner wasting all this lovely breathing time, waiting on my pesky balance to approach some kind of equilibrium and allow me to walk a straight line again. Equally, though, I couldn't see myself all at sea with Ulysses on his ship – that was a wave too far in my condition. So I did the next best thing and came up with a project that I could manage close to home: *999 Verandakus – A Memoir of Now,* in which I would post one Verandaku each day on Veranda Life, along with an accompanying image, for the next 999 days.

I would create, literally, a memoir of my Now, a record of moments in my life that I would observe, live and record, in the form of small poems with images.

I could manage that. It would be relaxing (once I got started), and I could take tea breaks.

It wasn't random, I realised, the veranda, the notion of writing poetry in the form of adapted haikus, the need to relax into something that wouldn't result in a comatose foetal position with nothing to show for it; and there was the drinking of tea, blessed, lovely tea. After all, when humans are in the midst of unpleasant times, bad and sad times, we tend to seek comfort.

What comforts you, dear reader? Think about it. Start now, since we're talking/reading/writing about it. Write a poem about comfort, perhaps a verandaku. Don't be afraid. There are no failures, only experiments. But how do you do it? Do read on – a convenient guide of sorts is coming up. Meanwhile ...

... here's a little story, a vignette, about something that I have found brings me comfort and has done so for a very long time ...

Verandas, and Veranda Life ...

... because my name is Jay and I'm a Veranda Lifer (and Lover, for that matter). There are many millions of us out there and we love verandas large and small for as many reasons, and more. Veranda Lovers can be excessive, it's part of their charm. You are obviously a charming veranda lover, too, grasshopper, otherwise why would you have read this far? (Oh, yes, perhaps the book's a gift, or you're reading the ebook version and it happens to be free at present – well, that's okay, too, as long as you're enjoying yourself – you are, aren't you? Of course you are, yes. Veranda Lovers also like to entice potential veranda lovers into the lifestyle, in case you hadn't noticed).

So, how did I come to be this way? It may have its roots in childhood, wherein my tea habit also began, sitting upon the knee of my Uncle Pat as he fed me sips of his strong black tea from the saucer of his tea cup. He lived next door, you see, and there was a gate in the dividing fence, a gate through which I toddled as a two-year old to visit Uncle P. and Aunty Nellie, lured as I was by that very special taste and scent of tannin wafting through the dawn breakfast hour before he went to his butcher shop – does it sound better in French, his *boucherie*? – to sell chops and bacon. Mmmm, bacon.

But back to the veranda. I grew up on one until I was about eight years old. I lived at one end of the veranda at the front of our house (closed in, naturally, and protected against the weather and most mosquitoes) and my brother lived at the other end. My brother's bedroom 'wall,' separating it from the rest of the veranda (and me at my end) was made of pegboard sheeting, and mine was half fibro and half louvres (allowing a great view of the TV in the lounge-room – I saw more episodes of *Peyton Place* than my mother could have imagined).

I loved veranda life as a child. I gazed out the front door while lying in bed and watched the passing parade of town loonies, sorry, luminaries, on their way to work and other confining spaces.

Life since then has been a series of verandas here, there, and yes, over there, except when it wasn't. These days, I'm glad to say, I write on my veranda whenever I like – I wrote an entire novel there a while back (time is elastic on the veranda, so forget about dates).

The other point to note here is that verandas bridge the gap between the outside and the inside, between being an outsider and being an insider. When you're a Veranda Lifer, you can look within and without, a valuable place to be in a world of complexity and confusion, don't you think? I've never felt entirely comfortable either entirely in or entirely out, so it makes sense to waltz a little and enjoy the veranda shuffle. And, as a bonus, it's the metaphor that just keeps on giving.

Which brings me to how it happened, and in retrospect, I can give credit to ...

S.M.A.R.T. Goals ...

... though I didn't quite know it at the time I planned and began to live T*he Verandaku Project*. Now, don't run screaming away from this section, it could be very useful for you, you never know, and it won't hurt (not much). Let me say that they (the goals) must have been rolling around in there somewhere with the vestiges of my abandoned public sector career (though, really, it was more a case of the other type of career: an uncontrollable lurch downhill) hiding among the synapses. S.M.A.R.T. Goals are Specific, Measurable, Achievable, Relevant, and Timely. You'll see them with slight variations in the words used but they'll give you the same outcome. And they're not the exclusive preserve of business or science or technology, the mean, hoarding devils – they belong to all of us and, essentially, they're simply reminders of what we already know and do instinctively every day as we negotiate our lives: we plan all kinds of stuff all the time and then we do it. Take a gander at the following illustration – I made it especially for you. Well, it's on the next page, and it's coming right up anytime now, okay, because I didn't want it to be squished at the bottom of this already pretty full leaf. I mean, just consider this rather long paragraph. Lengthy much. Meanwhile, take a moment to contemplate your breathing as you kick your shoes off and sink gratefully into your mid-century modern three-seater with a nice cup of tea, your half of the citrus tart you bought this morning after you finished the wretched grocery shopping, and the unfinished Scrabble game from last night.

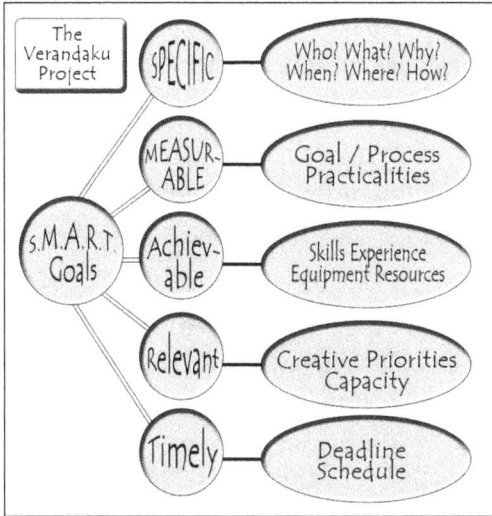

Here's a run-down of how S.M.A.R.T. Goals applied to *999 Verandakus,* and remember that in retrospect, I can be clearer (and cleverer if I play my words right) about it all and understand how unfolded. Feel free to use them for your own project. There's plenty on offer on the web about S.M.A.R.T. Goals if you need more information. Take it away, SMARTy-pants.

S.M.A.R.T Goal 1: *Specific*: you need to define your goal as clearly as you can and in some detail, or as much as you can muster at the start. So think about a creative project that you'd like to undertake. It doesn't have to be some big-time thing – something small or medium-sized will do the trick. Something you can incorporate into your life, however you're living it at the moment, and it needs to be something you feel fairly confident you can sustain. Then, ask the six questions:

Why, What, How, When, Where, Who? Let's look at them in turn (because taking turns is a laudable habit):

WHY?

In the case of this project, I wanted, and needed, to do something creative and there were a number of reasons, including:

- saving my sanity – I was sick and had limited mobility, not a happy mango madness, this much was certain (plus, I've never claimed sanity as a strong suit);
- the challenge – I wanted to continue to be creative because I'd been writing professionally for a couple of decades at this stage, and in any case I'd been writing both poetry and prose since childhood, and I would continue to write even though I was physically and geographically confined (though certainly not in a pregnant sense, no, no);
- focussing on something worthwhile – a creative project would require focus and attention, and yes, mindfulness and, if it could take me away from worrying about whether or not I'd ever get my balance back completely, then it was a good and worthy thing to do.

Having a worthwhile purpose for doing something, rather than a passing fad or fancy, is a built-in motivator when things get tough and you don't want to do it anymore (and you know, in the end, the tough get going, so suck it up, you tough little butternut pumpkin, you). So now, take some time to think about this little three-letter question-y word, grasshopper – why? It will both stand and seat you in good stead.

WHAT?

What do you want to do? As a writer, it was something of a no-brainer: I'd write. But what would I write? I began a novel which became *Spawned Secrets*, but the payoff for that project was different in its nature. Plus, it was ongoing in the sense that, while I had the satisfaction of completing chapters every day or every other day, the entire novel was more of a marathon, whereas poems, even those that would form a bigger project, were sprints: short, self-contained, and offering a happy dose of endorphins with the joy of each completion (have you noticed that sprinters seem to appear altogether happier, friskier and bouncier than dour, sketchy-looking marathoners? Not that there's anything wrong with that, the dour, sketchy thing).

Furthermore, and as a minty-fresh bonus, I'd written arguably thousands of haikus when I was a teenager and into my twenties. I remembered that I'd loved them for their brevity and the challenge of the form, the Westernized form, that is, of a three-line poem with 17 syllables in a 5-7-5 format. (If you decide to write Verandakus, you can check out the basic guide later in this essay). Somehow, that confining structure was very appealing in itself. Perhaps it was because of the nature of my own confinement – if my physical condition was controlling me, then I wanted to control something, too. And I wanted to make it my own, hence, the Verandaku: a haiku structure (*element one*) for mindful observations in the moment (*element two*), but without the traditional *third element* of the haiku form: a season word or phrase (words and phrases that suggest summer, autumn, winter or spring, such as leafless trees, warm days, blooms).

The other element I decided to add, as a nod to the visual nature of our contemporary culture, was an accompanying photograph to each poem, to either illustrate more about the poem, or to simply offer another mindful observation in image form. Digital cameras are cheap, the software is easy to use, and the internet loves pictures. Plus, I can't draw. Done and dusted.

So, what do you want to do, my friend? What would you like to accomplish creatively, inspired by *The Verandaku Project*? For one thing, think about what you *can* do, and compare it with what you'd *like* to do. Get yourself a sheet of paper, and create a mindmap. Draw a circle in the centre and choose your 'what.' It might be haiku, or photography, or music, or art. Then draw circles further out from the centre circle and fill them with more specific words. If it's a general subject like photography, your surrounding circles might contain words like 'landscape,' 'macro,' 'portrait,' or 'nature.' if you can be more specific, all the better. If haiku is your centre, then you might write 'garden' in one circle, 'animals' in another, 'weather' in another. You get the drift. Along with those circles, you might draw another and write 'elements' inside, then connect that via three lines to the three basic elements by writing: 'structure (5-7-5),' 'the moment,' and 'season.' Why not add 'My Elements' to signify that you'll be adding your own preferences? Take a look at the mindmap below to get an idea of how you can visualise the 'what' of a creative project.

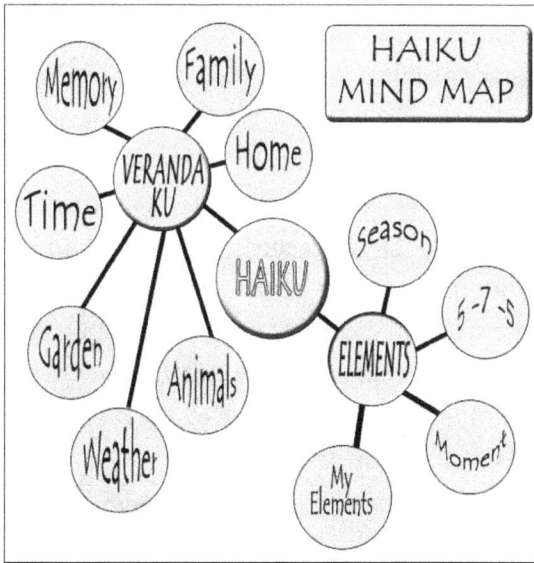

Such maps then allow you time for consideration and further research, including ...

WHERE? WHEN? HOW? WHO?

Yes, exactly where, how, and when can and do we engage with our creative selves? And with whom?

When I decided to begin *The Verandaku Project*, the **WHERE** wasn't an issue for me, as the boundaries of my physical condition had already been imposed. So, my immediate environment became the where, the natural, the only locale for the project and in that respect, it reminded me of a quotation paraphrased from Marcel Proust's *Remembrance of Things Past*: "The real voyage of discovery lies not in seeking new landscapes but in having new eyes." And I suggest that perhaps you could use this quotation as a guide to your own 'where.' You really don't need to go very far, and you don't need that many subjects. And if you do go far simply because you can, then identify a point of focus, a topic, a subject, an activity. My environment began with my own home and garden, my family and friends, my cats, my memories emerging in mindful moments, to be lured into, and to connect with the now. The sky and clouds above me changed all the time and all I had to do was look up. Initially, I could walk for only a few minutes a day, but gradually that built up over time as I felt less like a dizzy blonde (I can say that, I am somewhat blonde, but woe betide the non-blondes who try it on, baby). More of my streets became available and eventually we could take short trips to the nearby beachside suburbs and the botanical gardens, the museum and the art galleries. It was a gradual process, but it happened, and I took my camera with me to record those moments, inspired by Henri Cartier-Bresson, the pioneering French photographer, who put it this way:

> There is nothing in the world that does not have its decisive moment, and the masterpiece for good conduct is to recognize and seize the moment. If you miss it in the revolution of states, you run the risk of not finding it again or of not perceiving it.

All the more reason, grasshopper, to make friends with the present moment, whatever creative project you decide is most wonderful for you to embark upon.

Which leads me to **WHEN** I would be able to observe, reflect, and record my Verandakus. When would the decisive moments occur? For me, the right time was any time I could lure an observation or impression from the moment and (most of the time) clarify it through the lens of the camera, but more especially through the 5-7-5 three-line structure of a Verandaku. For that one needs mindfulness, your mind on the job of being in the present. I've found that many of my Verandakus come frolicking along when I'm out walking, but they can as readily offer themselves as I stand at the kitchen sink, or sit on the back steps watching lizards or an approaching shower, or talking to the graves of my departed cats (they're under thick, green and flourishing grass, mown regularly). The point is to make friends with the moment you are in, the only moment you're ever going to be in: this one, now. And after you've made friends, walk or sit, allow the moment to be your focus. What is there? Is it the wind, or lack of it? Is it parrots chattering in the bottlebrush tree? The sound of your shoes as you step from grass to gravel to bitumen. What are the clouds up to? Are they skittish, or heavy, thick and textured, or pillowy, scallopy, or broken up and pushed around by gusty bullies? And what does that aroma of garlic and barbecued beef remind you of? Then, you gently work the observation of the moment into your 5-7-5 form. It may happen like this:

Make a cup of tea
Breathe, relax, sip and watch for
your ku to arrive

HOW you go about your creative project is for you to decide, but if you've been involved in creative work before, you'll know that you need to keep a record of your ideas, and the best way to manage that is the simplest way: always carry a recording device of some kind with you: a digital recorder, a phone, a notebook and pen, a Babel cat with a photographic memory (strike that last one, that was wishful thinking by a curious cat owner). And in the case of *The Verandaku Project*, I took my camera with me as well as a notebook and pen. Don't think you'll remember the brilliant idea, the lovely phrase, or the perfect few inspirational words once you get home – you won't. Take it from one who knows (sob).

If you want to take advantage of the internet's offerings, and who doesn't, create (there's that word again) a blog on Wordpress, or Blogger, or Tumblr, wherever you feel comfortable, and share your productivity with the world. This is what I decided to do with *The Verandaku Project*. I began the Veranda Life blog with a vague notion of it being a place to share meditative and mindfulness practices, but the idea of *999 Verandakus* became appealing very quickly. Alternatively, keep your blog private and share it with yourself, or invited friends and family – Wordpress allows for a privacy option – and that brings us to **WHO**. Who is involved in this work of yours? Are you a lone creator? Are you a couple? Or a team, a family, a gaggle of friends? Verandakus are a rather solitary occupation, but you can most certainly share the spoils of your mindful momentary art. In fact, the images on Veranda Life are a combined effort (thank you, Lorrie, most deeply).

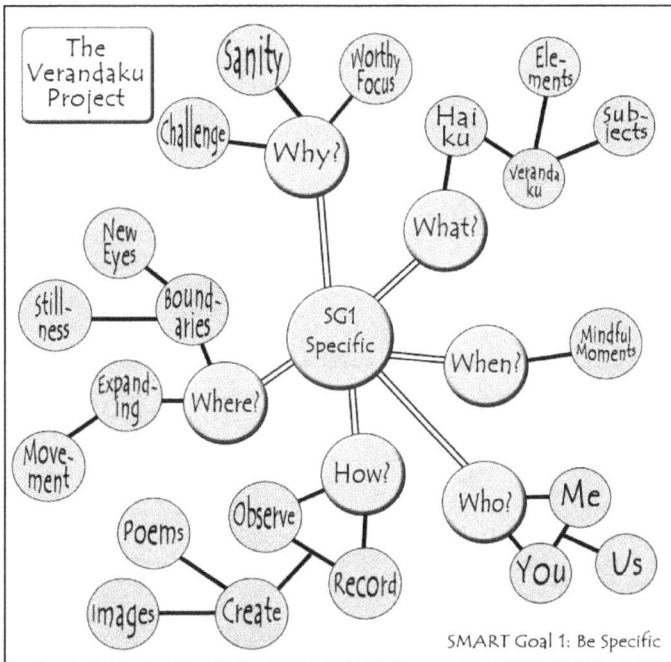

SMART Goal 1: Be Specific

Putting all of this together gives us S.M.A.R.T Goal 1: Be Specific.

And being specific is what the rest of the S.M.A.R.T. Goals demonstrate. You can get as specific as you wish, but I like to err on the side of simplicity if possible. Also, since I write Verandakus, and they're meant to be paragons of simplicity (and clarity), simple is good.

S.M.A.R.T. Goal 2: *Measurable:* businesses may need to include financial figures with their assessment of this goal, but all I needed to keep in mind for *The Verandaku Project's* measurability were my goal and how I'd proceed towards it: 999 Verandakus consisting of a poem and an image to form a

17

daily blog post. So simple, here's a little mindmap with just a few handy circles:

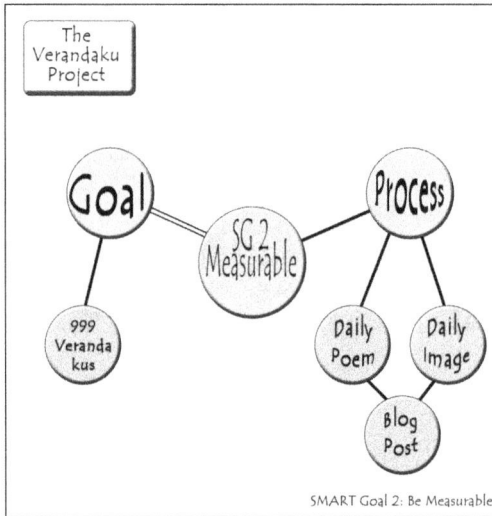

The Verandaku Project

Goal — SG 2 Measurable — Process

999 Veranda kus

Daily Poem   Daily Image

Blog Post

SMART Goal 2: Be Measurable

Unless you're planning a sizable creative project, perhaps you can keep your Measurables to a single goal and a fairly uncomplicated how to get there. With too many variables, a project has the potential to become cumbersome, and onerous. Cumbersome and Onerous isn't a firm of incompetent solicitors (but if you see a sign that says *Cumbersome & Onerous, Solicitors and Conveyancers,* avoid them at all costs, or it *will* cost you, grasshopper), they're what will put you off continuing with and achieving what you may come to think of as your heart's desire. Which brings us neatly to ...

S.M.A.R.T. Goal 3: *Achievable:* here's an interesting thing, actually describing all the elements of your project that will help you decide whether or not you need to tweak your goal or revisit your process. These S.M.A.R.T. Goals aren't meant to be linear, by the way. Probably that's another reason they really are smart, apart from the clever-dick acronym. You can quickly map them out and look at them side by side to give yourself a realistic idea of your project, its size and what you need to achieve its aims. *The Verandaku Project* was helped somewhat by my existing physical limitations and boundaries, so I confined myself to elements I already possessed and which I summarised as skills and experience, plus time and equipment.

SKILLS AND EXPERIENCE

I've been a professional writer for over 20 years, and a writer since childhood (I refer you particularly to my pot-hook and fish-hook musings, aged four and a bit). Plus, I have writerly qualifications of the academic variety, for what they're worth. No-one can magically make you a good writer, but you can learn an awful lot through reading and research and having mentors and colleagues to call upon. When I say no-one can make you a writer, my belief is that there needs to be some kernel of an innate or inborn gift waiting to be aroused and stimulated and taken to the next level (or at least to a party), and the next, as with music, for instance. My parents hoped I'd be musical (my mother was a fantastic violinist), but despite years of piano lessons, I was barely capable of getting a tight smile out of the ivories, let alone a tickled-up laugh, and I ditched the lessons as soon as I could. I love music, though, and I appreciate the fabulous musicians whose work I listen to every day. It's simply not something for me to create but rather to enjoy (come on down, Leo Kottke, Django Reinhardt, Sidney Bechet, Peggy Lee, Ella Fitzgerald, John Coltrane, Stephane Grappelli, the Dave Rawlings Machine, and all you others pushing up the back there).

But writing is something I want to create, perform, and do, as well as read and enjoy: there's some other motivator at work there and there'll always be a little bit of mystery about it, which is why this perspective of a level of innateness might be contentious and contestable. On the other hand, that's okay, that's entertainment, too. As is photography, an area of interest since childhood, and now that it's gone digital it's also something many of us who come from working-class backgrounds can afford to dive into far more deeply than when film and developing laboratories were the norm, and expensive (my first camera, though, cost forty-five cents, its first image: my mother impatiently standing outside the kitchen of our pub, carving knife in hand, giving me the *hurry-up or die* stare – well at least she came out, and I have her forever there, captured in *sternus momentus*, as it were). So, for the last five to seven years, I've been acquiring more (digital) photographic skills and taking photographic safaris and studying how to make Photoshop my friend. And I've done it in tandem with a fellow photography tragic (you know who you are, Lorrie), many of whose wonderful shots appear on the blog.

TIME
Speaks for itself, really, doesn't it? No? Okay. Occasionally, people who know I'm a writer approach me with a statement

that goes something like this: *I'm going to/want to write a book.* And I say, *That's wonderful – when will you start?* And they say, *I have some great ideas.* And I say, *Have you written them down so you don't forget them?* And they say, *Oh, no, not yet.* And I say, *Why not set aside some time every day, or maybe five days a week, or on the weekend, to quietly think about your story. Write down those ideas, work out a plot, consider who's your protagonist, what's your subject – those things.* And they say, *But I don't have time.*

You know where this is going, don't you? Yes, you do. We all have the same amount of time in a day – there's 24 hours (conspiracy theorists will tell you it's actually 26 and two were stolen by the government, however, I have it on pretty good authority from Greenwich that it's 24, but hey, up to you).

We can't save time like we can save money, or dingbats, or sugary screaming habdabs. It's here, time, now and now and now. We can determine priorities and schedule activities and then life gets in the way. I've found through experience that, on average, things take around twice as long to do as you think they will. Even so, I live in hope and, seriously, if you don't schedule, getting things done is that much harder. If you can incorporate even as little as 15 minutes into your day, within which you devote yourself to your creative project, you will achieve things, piece by tiny piece. Like exercise and hip fat, it's cumulative, so write it in your diary, put a box beside it, tick the box when you're done and feel the sense of accomplishment.

EQUIPMENT

Do you need anything else? Let's hope not, but if you do, be specific, determine the need, and find the most appropriate item to fulfill it. I mentioned earlier that I stuck with the resources to hand and they came down to a notebook (and pen), a camera, and relevant technology: my computer, internet access, and with the internet access a domain name and a hosting provider for my blog. Your creative project may not need technology as such, but *The Verandaku Project* was specifically designed to go online. These elements of S.M.A.R.T. Goal 3 are summarised below:

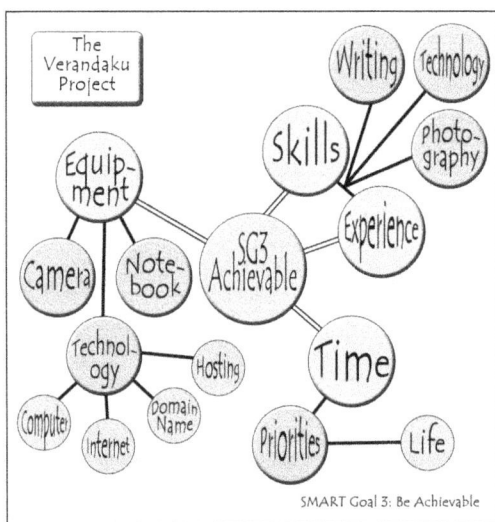

SMART Goal 3: Be Achievable

S.M.A.R.T. Goal 4: *Relevant*: By which I mean, we have to ask ourselves if our creative goals are worth the effort. Take yourself back to *why?* and consider how far you've come in terms of describing what you plan to do and how you'll do it. Are you still interested, champing to get on with it? Does it fit in with your other creative activities, or is this the first one? If so, could it become part of something wider, deeper, bigger? Or is it simply a one-off desire to undertake a creative activity with its own life? Is it a priority? One of several? List them.

When I began *The Verandaku Project*, I somehow knew (don't ask me how) that I'd finish it, leaving aside the possibility of death or some other peskily non-negotiable obstacle intervening. Years ago, you see, dear and gentle reader, I made a vow to myself that if I stated clearly to myself or others that I was going to do something, whether it be creative, academic, domestic, or otherwise, I would do everything in my power (with my ineffectual little fists [thank you, Dr Derek Shepherd and Shonda Rhimes] at the ready to brook no opposition) to finish it, reach nirvana, summit the peak, tick the box. This happened because I was terrified of being labelled a 'gunner,' by which I mean 'gunner do this, gunner do that,' as in 'gunner' equals 'going to' but never actually doing. Quaint Australian, and for all I know, global slang. Let's just say there's something of a history in certain quarters of my familial group to leave things undone, even half- or un-begun as it were, though such things may have been spoken of often and with the full intention of beginning and completing.

Sometimes when you make a vow to yourself, the thing you've vowed becomes (joyfully) embedded, internalised and real. It's a thing, as they say in the most articulate realms of the universe (especially that bar in *The Hitchhiker's Guide*

23

to the Galaxy). Consider such a vow, dear hearts, at least consider it – you never know how it may help you in the future, and now. My creative priorities revolve around writing primarily, and photography closely nearby as an activity integrated with writing, and standing on its own. They are, of course, central to *The Verandaku Project,* and can be summarised quite simply in the following illustration:

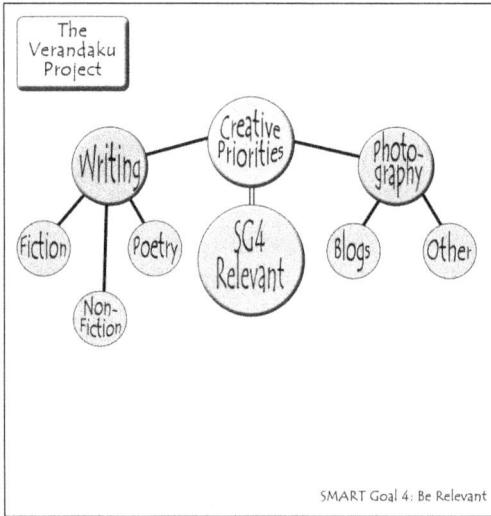

SMART Goal 4: Be Relevant

We're almost done, grasshopper, so let me present to you a simple, final letter, the letter 'T,' for ...

S.M.A.R.T. Goal 5: *Timely:* Indeed I do mean deadlines and time limits, and commitments (public ones are more effective than private ones, according to some researchers). There are countless millions of us poor schmucks who've tried and failed so often to conclude an activity, and notwithstanding the vow I took to finish the things I begin, sometimes finishing involves the heart-breaking decision to abandon a project that simply isn't going to do it for you in a trillion months of several trillion Sundays. That's a form of finishing in itself, though it may seem contradictory at first glance.

Be sensible. That's why S.M.A.R.T. Goals are there: to guide us through the morass of the potentially unfinishable and unworthy to what is definitely worth a vow and a shot. Tailor your goals to your bespoke project, as I did with *The Verandaku Project*. When you are as close as you can be to a creative endeavour because you've made a genuine commitment, you're so much more likely to do it. And once you've done it, there's a concrete motivation that's all yours to proffer as proof of artistry, and of the efficacy of your plan.

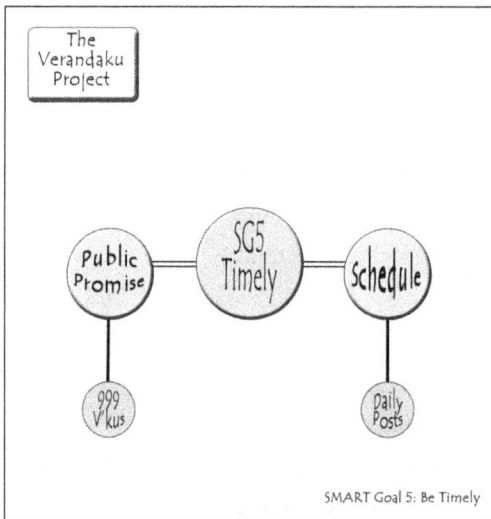

SMART Goal 5: Be Timely

Well, here we are at the end of the **S.M.A.R.T. Goals Guide to *The Verandaku Project***, and your own guide, if you'd like to try it sometime. And if you'd like to try it with haiku, or verandakus (and I certainly hope you will, and so do my cats since they're poetry in motion and have no need even of words), here it is now, fresh from a sell-out season at the big casino-y place in Las Vegas where only the loveliest guides perform ...

You Say Haiku, I Say Verandaku: A More or Less Teensy Guide (Relatively Speaking) ...

- o *Haiku* is an old, old form of Japanese poetry.
- o It emerged from another form – linked poems, and was initially called *hokku*.
- o It had some quite strict rules that we won't worry about here.
- o Suffice to say, traditional *haiku* involves those three basic elements we discussed earlier: it's of the moment, it references the seasons (nature), and it has a particular syllable count.
- o Its syllabic count is a different kettle of vowels in Japanese.
- o The Western version goes with a 5-7-5 format in three lines.
- o Some poets write even shorter poems with a count well below 17 syllables – hooray for them, too (check out my Zen Kettle blog where I write Zenkus, the daughters of Verandkus).

- *Haiku* is apparently simple, but also a challenge. There's always a catch.
- Many *haiku* poets rewrite their poems over the course of years, offering different versions of the originals. This can be a lot of fun, and also somewhat worrying of you happen to be a little bit obsessive.
- Matsuo Basho (1644-1694) is probably haiku's most well-known exponent.
- Others include Yosa Buson (1716-1783), Kobayashi Issa (1763-1827) and the great woman *haiku* master, Chiyo-ni (1703-1775).
- Robert Hass put out a very nice collection titled, *The Essential Haiku – Versions of Basho, Buson & Issa*.
- There are a lot of quite excellent contemporary *haiku* poets. Richard Wright is one of my favourites (see *Haiku: The Last Poems of an American Icon* – it's a beautiful collection).
- You can Google 'contemporary haiku poets' and discover worlds within *haiku* worlds.
- American poet Jane Hirshfield has published an excellent Kindle Single about *haiku*, titled, *The Heart of Haiku*. Highly recommended and very cheap (if you don't have to also buy a Kindle to read it – or, just get the free app for your PC or tablet).
- *Verandaku* is derived from *haiku*. It's a daughter of haiku, an inspired, admiring, respectful daughter (mostly).
- It follows the Western 5-7-5, three-line format.
- *Verandakus* are of the moment, or at least that is what they attempt to be.

o They are about pretty much any subject, and that's another thing about this sweet poetic form: its so versatile, or should one say verse-a-tile ...

o ... Probably not.

o The best way to polish your haiku or verandaku writing is to read a lot of these little poems and write a lot more, and then read a lot more and write a lot more. You get the picture, grasshopper.

o Remember to pull yourself into the moment, observe what's happening around and within you – it's all about detail and, frequently, juxtaposition, or bringing seemingly disparate notions or ideas together to form a new whole. For example, as I write this I'm listening to jazz and because we've had storms this week, the following verandaku occurred to me:

In Dave Brubeck's world

the afternoon beats and swings

Musical storm front

o Last night, in some of its moments, it came to me that the cover of this book, which features the Shorncliffe Pier at yes, Shorncliffe, is about a most beautiful veranda, one linking earth and sea:

A pier is land's

veranda over water

Sensing origins

o From left field, a final point: according to Huna (the ancient Hawaiian spiritual tradition), the *ku* is the subconscious mind, so perhaps we can say that *Verandaku* is trying to tell us something, maybe this:

Jay Verney

Breathe your deepest breath
Relax into mindfulness
Drink black tea often

縁側句
VERANDAKU

Verandaku

縁側句

1-333

#1

A bird on the fence

Black and white and singing loud

Happiness warble

#2

Two lost dogs lope in

We pat, feed and water them

They leave with a wag

#3

In the beginning

Caves, lean-to's, tents, verandas.

Couldn't we stop there?

#4

We are radios

channelling soul energy

our bodies spacesuits

#5

Droplets fall and apread

on the fabric of my shirt

The rain beats me home

#6

After the noon walk

discard hat, sunglasses, keys –

veranda, tea, breath

#7

Twists and turns of hose

Loop water through the garden

The basil sweetens

#8

Faces sprout in yards

Shiny, smiling, fully grown

Election harvest

#9

Veranda cats watch

They imagine grass salad

The long run downstairs

#10

A fence like headstones

Open and blank waiting for

impressive tenants

#11

Ibis on the bin

digs deep for pre-loved morsels

before the homeless

#12

Morning shadows stretch –

telegraph poles cross the road

Think they're there to stay

#13

By the police car

I jay-walk for fun and laughs

He's inside at lunch

#14

Even in winter

we seek shade from midday sun

Tropical cold barks

#15

Busy library

Surrounded by thriving trees

Inside only leaves

#16

Once the lamb roast cooks

leave the oven door open

Used heat just as warm

#17

A sudden shower

Its' scent the only warning

The clothes almost dry

#18

The bottle brush shrubs

wait in the garden with hope

for bottles to brush

#19

At the Give Way, life

Wired-on flowers wilting

another day past

#20

On suburban streets

sometimes busyness relents

Sweet silent seconds

#21

The cherry-pickers

pick power at the pole top

Sparkling light bulb juice

#22

The first day of Spring,

Sun glow, bird screech, dog bark, breeze

My mother's birthday

#23

High-voltage line guards

flap like Tibetan prayer flags

Safety for the soul

#24

The lop-sided tree

grows thicker on its left half

scorning the traffic

#25

After the mowing

Chlorophyll scented buffet

for all feathered guests

#26

Nails in power poles

hammer home tales of pets found

or forever lost

#27

Searching for meaning

I discover verandas

Breathe, relax, drink tea

#28

White and yellow screech

Sulphur-crested cockatoo

on its way to work

#29

For moments, silence

Birds, breezes, cars, workers – still.

I hear my shoes

#30

Dinner and a pat

What more could a sweet cat want?

Brush, kiss, cuddle, brush ...

The Verandaku Project #30

#31

A blustery change

invites winter in to stay

Doors slam in its face

#32

Parrots stretch from trees

flying to other perches

Colouring my day

#33

At our local park

the summer tree lop begins

Danger grounded, chipped

#34

A surfboard paddler

strikes the shallows far out and

carries his ride in

#35

The papaya tree

drops green fruit over the fence

taunting passersby

#36

After winter rains

blue sky paints in from the west

The first coat smudges

#37

Hum of bees at work

Scent of jasmine flowering

Anticipate Spring

#38

I tell the kitten

a wary approach is best

with most visitors

#39

The pillar-box waits

for people to decide if

today is the day

#40

On some windy days

ocean air sweeps far inland

Fossils sniff their birth

#41

The park bench seats three

Its plaque honours a dead man

Comfort from beyond

#42

Ducks have left the pond

and flown to the park for brunch

Two friends eating out

#43

A watering can

sits waiting for its owner

Half empty, half full

#44

The sleeping dog lies

just where she was yesterday

Tail swish signals life

#45

When Spring showers start

clouds paint in pointillist style

followed by a wash

#46

A day at the beach

Sun, sea breezes, lunch and talk

Sleepy by sunset

#47

New blooms, shy at first,

invite Spring to take charge and

grow their floral stars

#48

On a rowdy walk

my thoughts won't settle, don't stop

The present escapes

#49

The painter's brush swipes

a weatherboard, two, three, four

White gloss glows and fades

#50

The Sunday papers

take so much longer to read

than fast-print week-days

#51

Uncurl your fingers

Spread your hands across your thighs

Feel them warm; be calm

#52

Bird on a wire tweets

It needs no technology

to tell its story

#53

The I who writes this

is not the I who is me

Who is it that thinks?

#54

Magpies rule the roost

on the corner where they feed

But full birds don't dive

#55

A smell from the past

Nana's chook mash on the air

Visiting spirit

#56

Tree shade seems cooler

spilling onto grass and me

Soft edges blur truth

#57

At the building site

a whistle signals changes

Hot tea, cold cuts, lunch

#58

Rain droplets on leaves

form twitching clubs of gossip

on the sun's misdeeds

#59

Birds of paradise

raise their beaks to the storm clouds

waiting for fuel

#60

Two birds out walking

decide on a yard for lunch

Al fresco dining

The Verandaku Project #63

#61

A magpie youngster

revels in footpath freedom

Mother singing watch

#62

A single leaf dropped

by a bird lies waiting for

its friends to drop by

#63

On a day of fires

the sun works hard to stand out

Our focus elsewhere

#64

Half-moon mid-morning

watching the sun rise and glow

Room enough for two

#65

Jacarandas start

their blooming months and announce

exam time mid-Spring

#66

A truck full of signs

rattles through suburban streets

seeking direction

#67

A marshmallow sky

stretches to the horizon

softening the day

#68

Just before the rain

the sky darkens, wind rises

There are silences

#69

Greeted each morning

by parrots with attitude

Their screech is my joy

#70

On the bowling green

bowls glide from hand to kitty

Black, green, black, green, white

#71

Leaves race down the street

as though their lives were elsewhere

The wind knows the way

#72

A car door leaning

against the fence – small flowers

gaze from its window

#73

A cat sets herself

among palm trunks – her outdoor

treehouse with a view

#74

No-one in our street

heard the tree falling but we

heard it sawn and chipped

#75

Luminous colours

greet me as I step outside

after days indoors

#76

Coiled cable lying

on the grass waits to connect

the rest of the world

#77

Darkening clouds chase

birds from trees and me through streets

The wind at our backs

#78

Jasper the lost cat

stares at me from his reward

poster – safe up there

#79

A white cat, statue

still, patient, waits for her prey

to join the tableau

#80

Empty fields, hot days

Football two seasons away

The grass laughs it up

#81

A mismatched lounge suite

sits on a shady footpath

turning runners' heads

#82

Standing in tree shade

I feel the leaves' cool essence

Air-blown and gentle

#83

Arching its spine to

the sun, a fallen palm frond

is sitting pretty

#84

A stand of bamboo

rises towards sun and moon

Growing its business

#85

Under night's cover

mushrooms grow from somewhere to

live a day with light

#86

On a higher branch

a magpie rests and watches

moment by moment

#87

At the market day

watermelon nursery

rolls by – summer bites

#88

My cat smells the cheese

draping my wheatmeal biscuits

Who can deny her?

#89

At the traffic lights

a tableau of silence for

seconds of pure red

#90

Absolute blue sky

The paler cold of winter

Cloudless and lofty

The Verandaku Project #91

#91

Buses create drafts

rocketing through the suburbs

Ticket free air-con

#92

Fog changes the streets

They soften, discard edges

We disappear

#93

On wind-gusting days

trees sound like freeway traffic

The rush standing still

#94

In my neighbour's yard

a cast-iron dining set

invites passing trade

#95

The priest awaits the

hearse's arrival since the

dead don't care for time

#96

The empty playground

entertains a single bird

resting on a swing

#97

Winter sale brings heat

Swimming pool shell arriving

Excavate Summer

#98

Hanging from a crane

the pool shell undulates in

an ocean of air

#99

Gone to ground, captured,

the pool, its water – becalmed

Is Spring warm enough?

#100

Park, dog, kids, and dad

juggling distraction, keys, phone

Ted E. Bear sleeps rough

#101

Reward the painters

with a compliment or two

Sincerity works

#102

Soldiers train and work

You see them in shops on breaks

Unarmed in public

#103

A frayed winter coat

grown thin from years of loving

An old friend goes cold

#104

Drink black tea often

on anyone's veranda

Breathe relax and sip

#105

Winter beginning

Torts Contract Criminal Law

Please learn something else

#106

Dogs bark at night here

Afraid of the dark, and us

By day they sunbathe

#107

A biplane above

Its banner an earthly quiz

Will she marry him?

#108

Out on today's walk

each step differentiates

because I notice

#109

Each step up the hill

is measured breath by breath by –

more fitness needed

#110

A car without plates

left on the street overnight

Abandonment sucks

#111

Silence in the sky

as a jet glides through low cloud

Landing brings thunder

#112

Today in my 'burb

so much industrial noise

All at once, boom time

#113

Two in the garden

Cat and servant watching life

Neither knows the hour

#114

The dog leads him out

Small, furry, ridiculous

Power in his paws

#115

The petrol station

hosts white cars at all bowsers

How many weddings?

#116

School kids in the park

fan out blue across the grass

Uniformed painting

#117

Each step a new one

though each feels familiar

New step family

#118

An old man's jumper

worn inside out to the club

tells me of lost love

#119

The tip of my shoe

a butterfly's helipad

Grey and white still life

#120

Rain on the roof tiles

sifts a soft rhythm for sleep

Hope for morning sun

The Verandaku Project #120

#121

"U-turn permitted"

Street signs offer a way back

Renouncing today

#122

A child on the road

running with joy, fearless

Others worry best

#123

After the night's rain

humidity joins the sun

Winter takes a bath

#124

Summer in July

is an odd fit in the South

Pool splash comes early

#125

The childrens' voices

leave the park on gusty winds

Energy takes flight

#126

The sky is spitting

Random shots hit birds, kids, me

We are spitworthy

#127 – Mower Man Suite: 1

The mower man stops,

waves me on, and strikes a match

Settling for smoko

#128 – Mower Man Suite: 2

Mowing public space

he ambushes random blocks

Was smoko, toke-o?

#129 – Mower Man Suite: 3

Mower man is bored

The blocks become his puzzle

He plans a surprise

#130 – Mower Man Suite: 4

On my walk back home

mower man stalking the park

Grounded skywriter

#131 – Mower Man Suite: 5

The ride-on mower

Modern mechanical gift

Grass and people shrink

#132 – Mower Man Suite: 6

Mower man is done

His throne idles quietly

Grass lies low, for now

#133

What do you think of

a signwriter who can't spell

His van's ad says so

#134

Roofing iron rests

after years at the top

Hard sheets on soft grass

#135

A speedy toddler

will outrun one parent, two –

until the last step

#136

Thin women run past

fat women running, who ask

'Were you ever me?'

#137

Old women walk fast

Arms and legs pumping fresh blood

Hearts in extra time

#138

Man bike string bookshelf

A long wooden tail rides home

to all lengths of tale

#139

Shadows shrink at noon

leaving their owners alone

to follow themselves

#140

A man walking home

carries wine casks in each hand

Balance found and lost

#141

When you grow older

time's no longer your lover

Revel in haiku

#142

On foggy mornings

corellas among the lost

White wings beat the mist

#143

Traffic lights stop us

I watch a dog stroll through red

Colour blind and free

#144

When tea is steaming

everyone dips biscuits

Who will admit it?

Jay Verney

#145

In between showers

Rooves and roads dry out, wind blows

Leaves shake room for more

#146

Storm water trickles

Dry gutters suck the harvest

as the sun fights back

#147

A stray dog joins me

and runs ahead, then behind

The ease of friendship

85

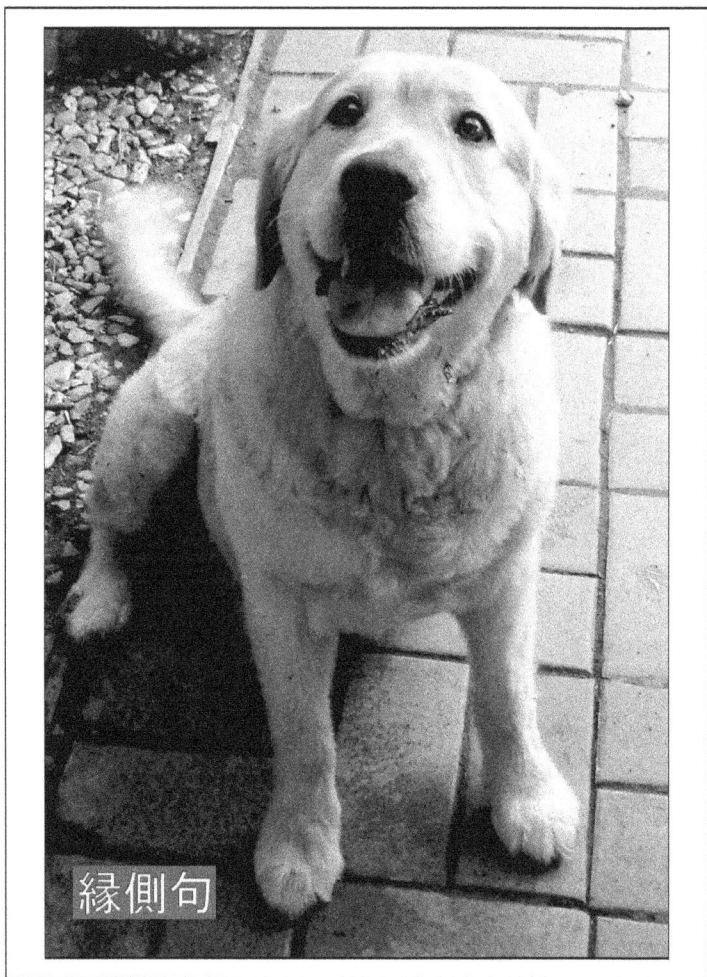

The Verandaku Project #147

#148

Pub patrons outside

with their cigarettes and drinks

Hostages to smoke

#149

Man with a snipper

walks the streets in search of weeds

Hinting at menace

#150

Flea market banner

shows the power of lost words

'Pre-loved tots and toys.'

#151

A coffee mug lies

near the gutter alone

Breakfast refugee

#152

A half-chewed apple

browning nicely on the grass

Waste or donation

#153

Usual suspects

run themselves from sleep to fence

Extra barks for luck

#154

Big man on small bike

His legs are pumping faster

than any street's length

#155

Driving one-handed

the man leans back, flicks fag ash

Sunday attitude

#156

Birds bend aerials

to suit their programming needs

They take the long view

#157

Lights on in the rain

drain batteries in the sun

Memory banks fail

#158

Moment by moment

predictability fades

And all is clear

#159

Turning the corner

wind drops and the heat rises

Different story

#160

In the clouds, thunder

and a plane's noisy engine

I can see neither

#161

A possum, three birds

and a nest in a tree don't

make ideal neighbours

#162

A scrub turkey strolls

down our footpath in the rain

Storm-lost but hopeful

#163

The house with no steps

waits patiently for footfalls

Ladders reach windows

#164

Magpies on the fence

Sunshowers lure worms topside

The birds sing and dive

#165

In freshly mown grass

the green scent of chlorophyll

dying for new life

#166

Wafting clouds up high

take their windy time to pass

The sun sees through them

#167

Magpies taking flight

sweep low, daring cars to speed

Chicken in bird world

#168

The Stop/Go sign man

tells both sides of the story

and is always right

#169

Parrots low in trees

Close enough, beak to mouth, for

exchanges of news

#170

Brick and timber rise

where ant hills used to flourish

Human ants arrive

#171

Gutters run for hours

after surprise winter storms

Tanks are tapped and tapped

#172

Darker clouds blow by

as white cumulus taunt them

to chase bluer skies

#173

Vacant lots look sad

They endure time, space, freedom

awaiting a home

#174

Branches on the ground

tell last night's stormy story

No need to make books

#175

Wreaths flower at ease

after yesterday's service

Night terrors recede

#176

Certain vantage points

show only roof- and tree-tops

Shaded lives beneath

#177

Tiny droplets fall

and make their surprising way

through thick canopies

#178

Travelling by foot

while my car is in the shop

I enjoy my speed

#179

Rain brings clarity

the day after running skies

Dust tamped, pollen drained

#180

Parrots screech dull days

into heat and bright colour

Chasing clouded sun

The Verandaku Project #181

#181

Tail wag and bark go

together in the dog who

can't tell if he's mad

#182

Scuttling in gardens

for the dark mulch of safety

A lizard's retreat

#183

News lies mouldering

in papers on the footpath

Read all about it

#184

Tree shade falls across

a road that used to be bush

Shadows favour all

#185

Entering the street

enveloped by sun, sky, breeze

Home away from home

#186

Rainbow lorikeets

feed and screech in bottle-brush

Camera-shy stars

#187

Do not think of life

as the be all and end all

Let it flow, relax

#188

Fog waits for the sun

to warm it through to sheer mist

The palest of skies

#189

Leaves blow across paths

sounding confident, as though

they know what comes next

#190

Friday's blooming tree

has lost every petal

by Monday – Spring speeds

#191

My clothesline turning

sounds like a sad, one-note flute,

determined to play

#192

You smell iron first

Then feel a drop, hear it

drumming up the street

#193

Two brown ducks glide in

Grounding themselves in stillness

before their park lunch

#194

After the weekend

footpaths and yards cut and cropped

Spring morning delights

#195

The scent of jasmine

fills the darkest night with the

sweet lure of comfort

#196

Sunset sea-breezes

spring from nowhere and surprise

our day's-end dreaming

#197

Water is finding

its level everywhere –

Spring rains come early

#198

A cockatoo flies

through white glare towards the sun

and disappears

Jay Verney

#199

Early morning dew

sits on grass in shining drops

bejewelled by sun

#200

Under Spring moonlight

A drunk fighting gravity

My father comes home

#201

Cicada resting

on the hand that saved it from

a footpath of feet

#202

On collection day

former furniture grandness

embraces nature

#203

Early morning ride

Cyclists pursue each other

seeking extra breath

#204

Mushrooms grow at night

and surprise our morning walk

past the neighbour's lawn

#205

Letterboxes wait

They are indifferent to

all deliveries

#206

Valentine's Day is

also my father's birthday

Love spills beyond dates

#207

A hot-air balloon

advertises real estate

The sky bought and sold?

#208

A rising jet trail

fights currents and gravity

on the way to – air?

#209

Summer twilight moon

lights a last half-hour of play

between work and dreams

#210

Leaves pressed in concrete

creating modern fossils

Instant history

The Verandaku Project #210

#211

Empty streets at dawn

are memories of absence

when peak hour rushes

#212

An abandoned van

free of parking rules at last

Askew from the curb

#213

When the burn-offs start

the air chill begins to wane

Summer in the smoke

#214

Magpies sing the trees

teaching their fledglings the tunes

that will save their lives

#215

The wind blows leaves up

from the road and down from trees

Unity in death

#216

On shady footpaths

timber waits to stand again

How lively this time?

#217

Someone's sweet perfume

drifts in early morning streets

After-shave competes

#218

A car driving past

squeaks out every wheel turn

Secondhand love call

#219

The soles of my shoes

contact mysterious worlds

with every step

#220

After the rain, blue

sky, a windless, clean today –

white clouds painted on

#221

Butterflies, knowing

it's Spring, cavort shamelessly

with us as we walk

#222

New names, fresh pages

Phone books: shrink-wrapped, weather-proofed,

await old readers

#223

Before you arrive

our cat strolls to the front door

Anticipation

#224

After dark, the scent

of night flowers comes to me

A lover with gifts

#225

The frangipani

cut-out decorates the deck

and offers a view

#226

Dogs out for a lark

inspect other dogs' driveways

Home smells much sweeter

#227

Down the steepest hill

I feel the age of my knees

Otherwise, joyful

#228

A rainbow arrives

after weeks of flooding rains

Hope colours the sky

#229

When westerlies blow,

palm fronds wave and leaves quiver

Playing to their strengths

#230

Some Stop/Go guys speak

Others keep their own counsel

Shift change tells their tale

#231

Sunday afternoon

The smell of mown grass competes

with warm carrot cake

#232

An empty playground

anticipates movement and

laughs – children arrive

#233

Raindrops move the leaves

Each drop and leaf devoted

to one another

#234

Nasturtiums dawdle

their way towards the footpath

Their shadows beat them

#235

Cat's paw raised and flexed

is a furry white puffball

Sunlight between toes

#236

A single magpie's

warble sounds like many more

A one bird quartet

#237

If whales were music,

what do you suppose they'd be –

Cello notes, swimming?

#238

The retaining wall

fell with help from gravity

Rain trickled it down

#239

When I hear a

palm frond falling, I wonder

who is gardening?

#240

The wind chimes rattle

as August westerlies start

Annoying so soon

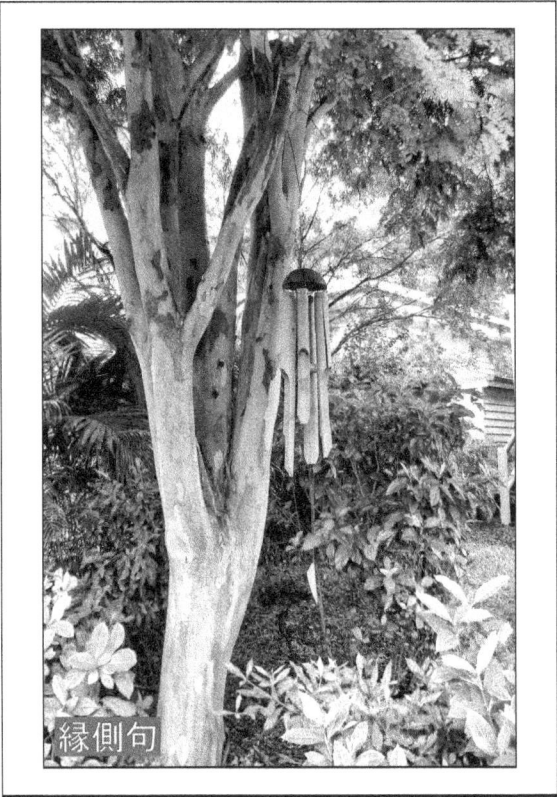

The Verandaku Project #240

#241

Man with a backpack

disappears in a blink

He's turned the corner

#242

In most of our yards

ants build empires inches high

Summer's rising damp

#243

After the deluge

gutters run like athletes in

search of a big race

#244

On the long walk home

seeing a woman I knew

Not stopping to talk

#245

Flowers bloom for Spring

I notice as they fall, stilled

near the front gate

#246

Every morning

trees leaf through musical notes

Violins hiding

#247

Bird beneath a tree

takes a shady rest and an

early morning tea

#248

Donut nibbled by

passing hungry birds and ants

Feast today, and then?

#249

Steps to nowhere can

tell stories of somewhere if

the right one passes

#250

Gardening chickens

peck the tastiest morsels

Their freedom short-lived

#251

The cat settles down

to watch her garden working

Lizards hurry past

#252

Showers on the way

Trees and flowers shimmy in

temporary sun

#253

A snail at full stretch

works its way across a leaf

Home relocation

#254

A scent of jasmine

drifts through diesel noise and fumes

Natural comfort

#255

Clouds and wind conspire

to steal and reveal the sun

Mystery logic

#256

Lemon-scented gum

offers balm to passersby

Childhood in a breath

#257

Gaggle of magpies

Beaks dipping, wings neatly tucked

Grounded for breakfast

#258

A pineapple slice

lies wilting on the footpath

Spiky defiance

#259

The paperbark tree

opens its leaves to the street

History lesson

#260

Cats imagine food

when they're sleeping and playing

Don't you think it's so?

#261

Moth on a window

Basking in background colours

Transparent still life

#262

Lost leaves on footpaths

lie flat beside lost branches

Low profiles for now

#263

Quivering flowers

reach up from their soily roots

Risky plant business

#264

Dead television

faces the street and the sun

Midday movie dreams

#265

Grass on the footpath

longing for the other side

No greener at all

#266

At the library

seeking the right book's comfort

Only one will do

#267

On hotter Spring days

cardigans are worn by the

elderly and drunks

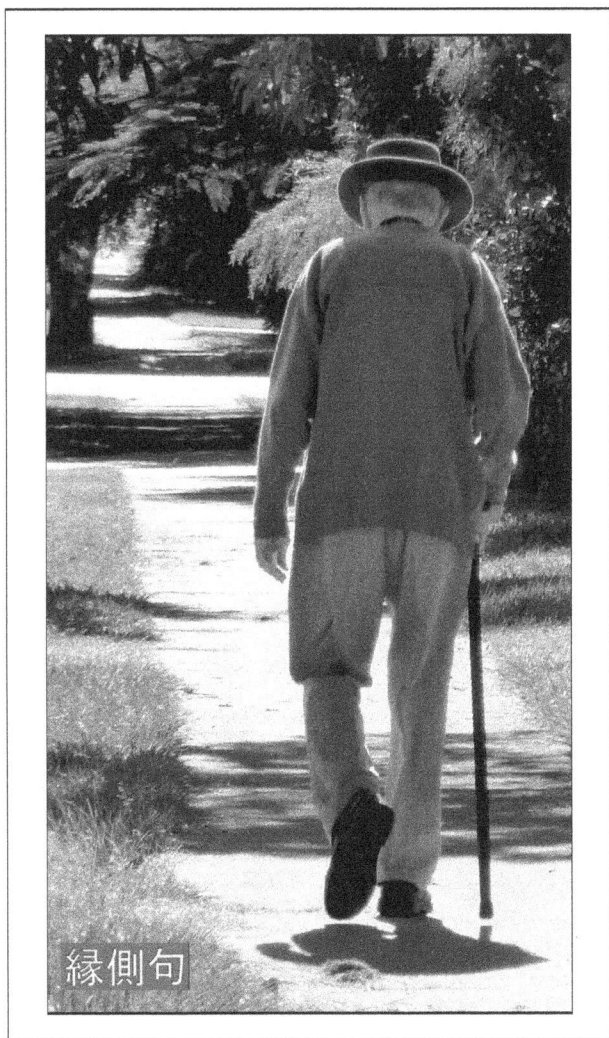

The Verandaku Project #267

#268

Discarded wrapping

lies on dewy morning grass

A surprising night

#269

Runners in lock-step

sharing the street's vibrations

Adding their rhythm

#270

News wrapped in plastic

Coiled and ready for eye strikes

Uncurling drama

#271

While youth supports you

enjoy each equal moment

They all count for now

#272

My cat follows dust

motes invisible to me

I watch her instead

#273

A very large chook,

red, plastic, floats above rooves

Take-away food sign

#274

A planter-box swan

filled with greenery and sun

Its flight path perfect

#275

Traffic sounds like the

sea again – must be time for

a visit with waves

#276

Sitting beneath the

shadiest tree, clouds arrive

to help me stay cool

#277

Listening to drums

my heartbeat joins the rhythm

Silence deafens me

#278

The smell of mown grass

lingers into evening

warming midnight air

#279

After Anzac Day

wilting wreaths beneath campaigns

There is room for more

#280

Discarded trolley

Sunbaking a novelty

Awaiting rescue

#281

On the way to school

children and mothers thinking

of different days

#282

The library's trees

shade their bookish relatives

Living inky dreams

#283

Leon's bench and tree

Silent invitations to

sit and wait a while

#284

Memorial walls

don't alphabetise the dead

Ranks thin randomly

#285

At the library

searching for just the right book –

Contenders galore

#286

Summer is long gone

but reminders appear

to raise our spirits

#287

Moving van full, kids

in the car, keys surrendered

They leave us for good

#288

An intersection

People, dogs, bicycles, cars

Each one knows a way

#289

Racing stripes on cars

ensure fast delivery

of some perceptions

#290

Wind on a fine day

brings a hint of winter's chill

Autumn playing games

#291

How good is this 'hood?

No wreaths have been vandalised

They're on self destruct

#292

In the intervals

between traffic burst and shrieks

I hear my breath

#293

A small dragonfly

watches cockatoos at play

Squab cares less, careless

#294

Lost bicycle chain

starts its new life as a snake

impersonator

#295

The tip of a pen

is more powerful than war

It is war's father

#296

Flowers stretch their stems

escaping their humble roots

without leaving home

#297

Around the corner

dead earthworms on the footpath

Late birds catch nothing

#298

Cracks in the pavement

Nature always finds a way

to outperform us

#299

Walking the footpath

I am welcomed by jewels

Leaf points in the sun

#300

Owners sunbaking

with their magnificent cars

Metal showing off

The Verandaku Project #298

#301

A lost luggage tag

left to its own devices

Where is it welcome?

#302

Early morning moon

fights the sun for attention

It needn't worry

#303

Kids, parents, teachers,

Organised footpath chaos

Lookouts keep their cool

#304

Jeffrey Smart's paintings

are here in the tin and brick

of my local streets

#305

A seabird arrives

to remind us of oceans

measured in wingflaps

#306

Chimney, antenna

Old and new converge above

conversation space

#307

The cold snap brings wind

and wafts of Vicks on the air

We follow the sun

#308

The garden of trees

went missing on the weekend

Stumps dream of new growth

#309

A little pink house

waiting for the one someone

who loves at first sight

#310

A march of tall shrubs

traps the morning sun's glitter

Temporary bling

#311

My cat on the deck

Her paws folded so neatly

Lizards think they're safe

#312

Container lid dropped

for soup, stew, dessert inside

I'm hungry now, so ...

#313

In the hill country

people know that what comes down

must rise again, too

#314

The path most travelled

is only slightly crooked

How easy the walk

#315

A pair of wet socks

fallen from a tradie's truck

Their life's purpose changed

#316

High cloud rolling in

changes today's colour and

brings its own silence

#317

Discarded ticket

for a game done and dusted

Memento of loss

#318

Foggy morning air

chills fingertips and aches bones

The sun layers off

#319

A slippery-slide

on its way from grandparents

A new history

#320

Winter chill blows in

Antarctica sends greetings

The sun cools its heels

#321

On our TV news

helicopters fly and swoop

They land nearby

#322

The monsoon drifts south

Rivers slide over their banks

and lazily spread

#323

Bushwalking in town

around the library's park

Reading nature's way

#324

Shadows change at noon

The afternoon shift hovers

leaning towards home

#325

Pine cone surrenders

to the footpath and awaits

opportunities

#326

The magpies and crows

set their own standards of play

It's all in the swoop

#327

Birds chase each other

from tree tops to power poles

Perches are perches

The Verandaku Project #326

#328

I step on an ant

without care – is it malice

or simple neglect?

#329

Some babies' cries sound

like tiny drop-saws through pine

Intent on cutting

#330

Wind buffets their sides

then turns and pushes behind

Air-mugging walkers

#331

Dog with a big bark

agitated as I pass

Fences make good walks

#332

Today the garden

floods and ants' nests overflow

New homes tomorrow

#333

The garden by day

A scene of earthly delight

Night secrets rustle

About the Author

Jay Verney is an Australian author who has published novels, essays, short stories, poetry, memoir, magazine and newspaper columns, book and film reviews, and comics.

Jay's first novel, *A Mortality Tale,* was shortlisted for the Australian/*Vogel* and Miles Franklin Literary Awards (and is available as both a paperback and an ebook). Jay has a PhD (in genre and crime fiction), and a Master's degree (memoir) in Creative Writing from the University of Queensland. In 2009, she received a Dean's Award for Outstanding Research Higher Degree Thesis for her PhD.

Jay's second novel, *Percussion*, is available in both ebook and paperback, as is her third novel, ***Spawned Secrets***. Her fourth novel, ***Summon Up The Blood***, is a result of her PhD and is also a paperback and an ebook, along with the essay that accompanied the novel, ***Creating A Custom Fit In An Off-The-Rack Genre World.*** Jay's memoir, ***The Women Come & Go*** includes an essay, ***The Women Came & Went,*** a reflection on writing the memoir and how writers research and re-imagine history and lives. It's available in, wait for it, paperback and ebook formats, too. Celebrate.

Visit virtual Jay at her websites for **free** entertainment:

Transient Total Focus – www.jayverney.net
One blink at a time
The mother ship, where minty fresh stuff and nonsense and even some useful things reside.

Veranda Life – www.verandalife.com
Breathe ~ Relax ~Drink Black Tea Often
999 lovely haikus with lovely images, and the inspiration for this book. All the images are there, too. Enjoy.

Zen Kettle – www.zenkettle.wordpress.com
It makes tea
Zenkus, teeny tiny haikus about life, the universe, and everything. Also lovely.

Last Cat On Mars – www.lastcatonmars.wordpress.com
Would you want to be the first?
Dr On Mars welcomes you to a comical world of fun and
laughs. It's laughly, and lovely, yes.

You can give Jay all your money by visiting Amazon to
purchase even more of her darling works. Ask Prof. Google
for 'Jay Verney Amazon.' You know you want to,
grasshopper.

If you enjoyed this book, please don't hesitate to *visit
Amazon and post a review*. The author will be so grateful,
she'll send you a picture of your very own avatar in
minifigure world posing with the Martially famous Last Cat
On Mars and also, a bonus ice-cream and naturally the
blessings of her mother's violin bow.

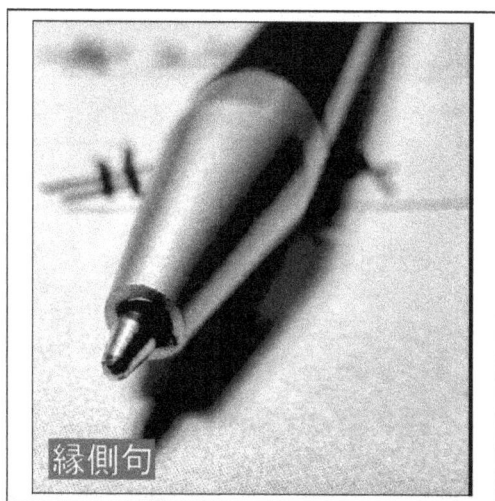

Your life in moments
Verandaku capturing
three lines at a time

www.ingramcontent.com/pod-product-compliance
Lightning Source LLC
Chambersburg PA
CBHW031548040426
42452CB00006B/238